Diving Boards & Trampolines

Vol. II

Diving Boards & Trampolines

Vol. II

88 Meditations to Launch You
Into Purposeful Living

Amy Layne Litzelman
www.AmyLayneLitzelman.com

Window of Worship Publishing

Diving Boards and Trampolines Vol. II
Copyright © 2015 Amy Layne Litzelman. All rights reserved.

No part of this publication may be reproduced, stored in a retrieval system or transmitted in any way by any means, electronic, mechanical, photocopy, recording or otherwise without the prior permission of the author except as provided by USA copyright law.

Scripture quotations marked (AMP) are taken from the Amplified Bible, Copyright © 1954, 1958, 1962, 1964, 1965, 1987 by The Lockman Foundation. Used by permission.

Scripture quotations marked (NIV) are taken from the Holy Bible, New International Version®. niv®. Copyright© 1973, 1978, 1984 by International Bible Society. Used by permission of Zondervan. All rights reserved.

Scripture quotations marked (NKJV) are taken from the New King James Version®. Copyright © 1982 by Thomas Nelson, Inc. Used by permission. All rights reserved.

Scripture quotations marked (NLT) are taken from the Holy Bible, New Living Translation, copyright © 1996. Used by permission of Tyndale House Publishers, Inc., Wheaton, Illinois 60189. All rights reserved.

Scripture quotations marked (ESV) are from The Holy Bible, English Standard Version®, copyright © 2001 by Crossway Bibles, a publishing ministry of Good News Publishers. Used by permission. All rights reserved.

Scripture quotations marked (NASB) are from The Holy Bible, New American Standard Version®, copyright © 1995 by Lockman Foundation. Used by permission. All rights reserved.

Published in the United States of America
ISBN: 978-0-9965098-3-1
1. Religion, Christian Life, Devotional
2. Religion, Christian Life, Spiritual Growth

"I have no greater joy than this,
to hear of my children walking in the truth."

III John 1:4, NASB

Introduction

During my college years I traveled with a group of friends to a lake house for the weekend. My friend's family owned a boat and they all loved to waterski. I, on the other hand, knew nothing about the sport. It came my turn to try and my heart swelled in my chest. I so longed to jump up and give it a go, but logic and fear rushed up to remind me, *"You don't even know how to swim! How are you going to feel when you make a fool of yourself?"*

I was wearing a life vest, my friends were willing to teach me, they were even cheering me on, but in a split second the words "No thanks" slipped out and deep regret replaced my longing. Before I knew it the weekend was over and my opportunity with it.

A point comes in every story when a decision must be made, a step taken, and a destination either pursued or abandoned to the silent ponderings of *"What if...?"* As anyone who has gotten stuck in the rut of fear knows, doing nothing *is* doing something. A prolonged pause is, for all intents and purposes, abandoning the pursuit. Sitting down at the wrong time can easily abort a journey and change the goal. *"Maybe next time..."* usually means *"Maybe never."*

Forward movement is essential for growth.

Being a disciple of Jesus is no exception. Jesus calls you to *follow* Him. To become like Him. To allow Him to live again on earth *through* you. This takes forward movement. Faith requires advancing motion. You might not know what you'll find or where you're going, but you must *choose* to take the next step if you want to continue the journey with Him. Only rarely do you fall forward by accident.

As with my waterskiing experience, all you need is in place: a lifejacket of grace is at hand to empower and uphold you; a mighty host surrounds and cheers you on; and the Holy Spirit is your Teacher leading to all truth. The only risk lies in saying, "*Maybe later...*"

While putting together this collection of meditations, the Holy Spirit prompted me with the title *Diving Boards and Trampolines*. I scribbled it down immediately, as it captures a higher purpose and essence of the book. Each reflection is an opportunity to explore, an excuse to try new ground, and a platform to launch you to new dimensions of relationship with Jesus and in life. The value of this book lies not only in the meditations, themselves, but where they will lead you.

Consider this: You would never set up camp on a diving board or build a house on a trampoline. They are not parking spaces, but launching pads, taking those who are willing to deeper depths and higher heights. Launching pads speak of possibility, adventure, and rewards.

In the same way, these pages are points of transition. They call for both thought *and* action.

Being a disciple of Christ demands you go forward yet more and more each day, into the glorious unfolding of your unity with the Trinity. This unfolding will not only reveal the majesty of your Maker, but your destiny and calling as His child, friend, servant, ambassador, priest, and bride.

You were created in Christ to search out hidden treasure and jump to higher ground. He calls you from faith to faith and glory to glory. Each new day holds the promise of a step forward. A step closer. A step deeper into the One who encompasses all you desire and hope for.

Russian author Fyodor Dostoyevsky may be accurate in his words, "Taking a new step, uttering a new word is what people fear the most." Going into the unknown can be very intimidating. Yet we were never meant to do this in our own strength and fortitude. Jesus sent us the perfect Guide and Helper, the Holy Spirit.

If you're like me, you may have this crazy idea that you're supposed to know how to do something *before* you do it. But Jesus has a very different perspective:

> *"I tell you the truth, anyone who doesn't receive the Kingdom of God like a child will never enter it"* (Luke 18:17, NLT).

I encourage you, come as a child. Come curious. Come expectant. Come with laughter and questions and the willingness to make mistakes along the way. Come and see and touch Him. Soon He'll capture your heart in new ways and you'll wonder why you waited so long to embrace such joy.

How to Read This Book

The reflections in this journal came in the movement of everyday life, while washing dishes and cooking dinner; driving to town or on a morning walk. They came in the flow of conversation with the Holy Spirit or as sweet interruptions to my day. They are meant to make one contemplate – and then create. To pause – and then pursue.

This pursuit will look different for each individual, yet carry a similar rhythm and fragrance. It's not about doing one specific activity or ritual, but building relationship – with your Creator, yourself, and those who surround your days.

Each meditation is followed by a blank page, ready for your input. Record scripture or journal observations; sketch thoughts or paste in pictures. There's no right or wrong way to use the space. However and whatever God choses to speak, pour it out upon these pages. Take the simple reflections I offer, pause, and then jump.

I chose to include a creative side to this journal as our God first introduces Himself as our Creator. And we, each one, are made in His image. Some of you may already express this trait in vast and varied ways. Others may not see yourself as having a creative nature at all – but you do! It's just waiting to be discovered.

I know because I have uncovered new dimensions of my creative side in the last year and I'll never turn back. How often we find what we've long desired in the very thing we avoid. We encounter the One who fills *all* with His glory – even us. What joy He brings to dry, dusty, dark corners. What color and light and beauty.

One note of caution: Getting to know God is not like a lap pool, but a vast, deep ocean and an endless mountain range.

- Take your time with each entry. (*Days, weeks, months, whatever it takes.*)
- Consider.
- Pray.
- Listen.
- Use other resources to expand your study.
- Worship with your pen, your pencils, your brush, your camera, your life.

We're on a journey of eternal proportions and the Author and Finisher of your faith longs for you to go deeper *in* Him and higher *with* Him.

- Permit truth to renew your mind.
- Expect new thoughts and ideas, new dreams and realities to take shape.
- Expect the fruit of God's Spirit to grow on you even as the Tree of Life.
- Step out and see His plans rise up to meet you.

The Kingdom of God is at hand, but only those who look for it will see. Only those who accept the invitation will taste. Only those who go beyond themselves will experience the destiny God has waiting.

> *Holy One, thank You for seeking me out; for inviting me in; for taking me on this journey. May anticipation rise up within to hear, to see, to know You even as I am known.*

(1)

In Christ you are a new creation – and He created you to finish well.

(2)

You are not alone.

God has put you on the hearts of others, some you've not yet met. Look around. Pray for them also. Get ready for when you will meet...

(3) If you feel distant from God, ask Him to teach you how to receive more of His love. It's never a question of His giving, but learning to welcome Him.

"Love me Lord like You want to do
So I can do what You ask me to."[1]

(4) Expectation is a lightning rod for God's presence and plans.

(5) God isn't intimidated by circumstances, but loves and heals the one who stands against Him in ignorance – and protects His servant in the middle.

Acts 16:20-34

(6)
It's never too late to be young.
Do something fun and creative today!

(7)

The Holy Spirit loves to open windows to God's heart. Just ask.

"But it was to us that God revealed these things by his Spirit.
For his Spirit searches out everything
and shows us God's deep secrets."
I Corinthians 2:10, NLT

(8) You were not created to be strong in your own effort – but in your union with Jesus. Your weakness is the point of potential for Him to demonstrate His strength.

"I have been crucified with Christ;
and it is no longer I who live, but Christ lives in me;

and the *life* which I now live in the flesh I live by faith in the Son of God, who loved me and gave Himself up for me."
Galatians 2:20, NASB

(9)
    To find the joy of obedience you must embrace the glory of humility.

(10)
"Saving grace, sweet fragrant grace
Like rain upon a thirsty ground
Upon me pour 'til I can hold no more
Come and fill me back again
Fill with Life again in You."[2]

(11)

Breathe deep.

Remember: Man's first breath was the very breath of God. You are His most precious creation.

(12)

To find that God is neither reduced nor manageable but altogether above and beyond you is to enter into the wisdom of the ages and the joy of His majesty.

> "'You are My witnesses,' declares the Lord,
> 'And My servant whom I have chosen,
> So that you may know and believe Me
> And understand that I am He.
> Before Me there was no God formed,
> And there will be none after Me.'"
> Isaiah 43:10, NASB

(13)

"Your tender mercies, God,
They stretch from earth to sky
And wrap me up in Your great plan
A plan too great… but here I am!"[3]

What does that look like today?

(14)
In great wisdom, God takes the very obstacle in your path and turns it into a bridge to reach your future.

(15)

Though the nations rage, Jehovah confidently tells you, "Be still and know that I am God."

"Those who live in the shelter of the Most High
will find rest in the shadow of the Almighty."
Psalm 91:1, NLT

(16)
You are not lost in a sea of faces. God has a good, very personal plan for you. Ask. Seek. Find.

(17)

God is still taking His children from prison cells into the King's court in a single day. Believe.

(18)

God's "Plan A" has never changed: He still wants to walk with you in the cool of the day.

Genesis 3:8-9

(19)

Godly wisdom may appear boring, even asleep compared to popular opinion. But at the right moment it flies swift and hits its mark.

"...wisdom is proved right by all her children."
Luke 7:35, NIV

(20)
    Following Jesus is a divine dance between grace and obedience.

(21)

It's not enough to buy the board. It's time to ride the waves.

"I tell you the truth, anyone who believes in me
will do the same works I have done, and even greater works,
because I am going to be with the Father."
John 14:12. NLT

(22)

Holy Spirit, be the wind in my sail today. Lead me to my Father – to my destiny.

(23)
Trusting in the unshakable God
will make *you* unshakable.

(24)
The beauty of a shadow: To remind you light is nearby.

(25)

Sometimes, to deal with the hurdle before you, you don't need to search for new truth or understanding so as much as live out what you already know.

> "...let us hold true to what we have already attained *and* walk *and* order our lives by that."
> Philippians 3:16, AMP

(26)
Be aware of who you choose to walk intimately with.

- Do you build one another's faith?
- Or feed each other's weaknesses?

(27)

One of the most important prayers you can ever pray: *Father, how do You see me?*

Ask often. His answers may surprise you.

(28)
Saturate yourself in the things of the Kingdom.

"Your kingdom come. Your will be done,
On earth as it is in heaven."
Matthew 6:10, NASB

(29)

What you don't yet understand with your mind can still be embraced by your spirit. He is leading you to all truth and grounding you deeper in His love.

> "And may you have the power to understand,
> as all God's people should,
> how wide, how long, how high, and how deep his love is."
> Ephesians 3:18, NLT

(30)   It is incredibly freeing to realize the goal has never been to prove to the world how amazing you are, but to be willing to be a vessel for your Creator to reveal how amazing He is.

(31)

In Christ, regret no longer need be a part of your life.
In His hands, nothing is wasted.

Redemption is beautiful.

(32) While others are making New Year's resolutions, why not ask God what *He* is resolved to do this year and how you can be a part of His plan.

(33)
>
> Deception is like a puzzle piece that fits the hole, but doesn't match the whole.

Truth and lies are not interchangeable
if you want to reach the correct outcome.

(34)
The words of God are eternal. No amount of erasing can stop them. Listen. What's He saying today?

Dreams.

Visions.

The Bible.

Friends.

Creation.

Audibly.

(35)
    Not every trail leads to Life.
        Choose wisely.
            Allow God to perfect your way.

"God's way is perfect...
He makes me as surefooted as a deer,
enabling me to stand on mountain heights."
Psalm 18:30; 33, NLT

(36)
Jesus.
Sometimes there are no words to describe Him…
and that's good.

(37)

What would change in your life today if you began to see it through the eyes of eternity?

"Then God opened Hagar's eyes,
and she saw a well full of water.

She quickly filled her water container
and gave the boy a drink."
Genesis 21:19, NLT

(38) Following Jesus has never been about what you can do for Him. Instead, it reveals the immensity of what He has already done and the miracle that, if you let Him, He will do much through you.

(39)

Perfection: not something we attain but are, simply by carrying His fingerprint.

(40)

Knowing where you are going is not so important as knowing Who you are going with.

"You go before me and follow me.
You place your hand of blessing on my head."
Psalm 139:5, NLT

(41)

Holy One, help me to not waste time. To recognize what's important. To see beyond logic to wisdom.

(42)
As you follow Jesus, majesty and intimacy merge in a way found nowhere else in the universe.

"For all who are led by the Spirit of God
are sons of God."
Romans 8:14, AMP

(43)
The very thing God gives you the passion to do is often on the same path you have to take in order to deal with your issues. Wise God.

(44)
What nobler thing could you ask of God than the humility to recognize His voice and the courage to follow…?

(45)

Many are the blessings you find when you stop searching for blessings and rest in God's love.

"Just as the Father has loved Me, I have also loved you; abide in My love."
John 15:9, NASB

(46)

Jehovah Bara made this day. It's not a fluke or mistake or twist of fate. It's not the idea or creation of another. And He is excited to unfold it to you!

> "Do you not know? Have you not heard?
> The Everlasting God, the Lord,
> the Creator of the ends of the earth
> Does not become weary or tired.
> His understanding is inscrutable."
> Isaiah 40:28, NASB

(47)
Need hope? Feast on Truth.

"And you will know the truth, and the truth will set you free."
John 8: 32, NLT

(48)
Your freedom and healing in Christ isn't so much about change in your circumstances as a change in how you see and know Him.

(49)
Truth always leads to joy – even if it goes through the valley of mourning.

(50) Don't try to live up to others' expectations – or even your own. Let Jesus pour Himself through you and live up to His!

"Now all glory to God, who is able,
through his mighty power at work within us,
to accomplish infinitely more than we might ask or think."
Ephesians 3:20, NLT

(51)
Sometimes the greatest compliment is silence.

The
Lord
is
in
his
holy
temple;

                                                       let
                                                      all
                                                      the
                                                   earth
                                                        be
                                                silent
                                             before
                                                  him.[4]

(52)

You aren't just another number.
He knows your name; your favorite food; what you say to yourself in the dark. He knows. He listens. He cares.

(53)

You are seated with Christ in heavenly places. Are you aware of it? Or do you only see the world around you? Get His perspective and bring it down.

"For he raised us from the dead along with Christ
and seated us with him in the heavenly realms
because we are united with Christ Jesus."
Ephesians 2:6, NLT

(54)

God speaks your destiny over you even before there's any sign of it; even before you believe it. Even when He knows you will fail many times before its reality.

> He believes in the power of His Spirit
> at work within you.

This is love.

(55)

You're not stuck in your weakness when you carry the Life of Christ within. Be who He says you are.

(56)

Hearing the voice of the One who created you – it's the sweetest of sounds. And it's for every day.

"Speak, Lord,
your servant is listening..."
I Samuel 3:9, NLT

(57)
Holy One, You leave me satisfied, yet hungry for more.

(58)

No matter what surrounds or overwhelms, there's open sky on the other side. Keep going.

(59)
Your Creator is in relentless pursuit of you...
to the ends of the earth,
to the ends of your heart.

And it's all for love.

(60)
Colors. Tastes. Sound. Texture. Fragrance. Imagination.
All glimpses of our Creator's passionate nature.

(61)

Natural and supernatural encounters – both reveal One who became a sweet aroma and calls us to the same.

"Our lives are a Christ-like fragrance rising up to God..."
2 Corinthians 2:15, NLT

(62)

Limiting your faith in Jesus to *life after death* is like sitting in a boat while it sits on the shore. Go ahead. Push off into the deep. Knowing Him in His element is what you were created for.

(63)
Stop a moment. Soak in the details...
It won't happen like this again.

(64)
　　Sunshine through the rain clouds –
　　There must be a rainbow out there somewhere!

"And his name will be the hope of all the world"
Matthew 12:21, NLT

(65)

Ask. Seek. Knock.

You'll never know for yourself until you do.

(66)

I love Mondays. They feel like a fresh canvas.

What are *you* going to paint this week?

(67)

If your King was coming to your home today, what gift would you greet Him with?

(68)

Every moment, every breath, every barefoot step on a cold floor and leaf blowing by – such treasures.

> "I will praise the Lord at all times.
> I will constantly speak his praises."
> Psalm 34:1, NLT

(69)
    Your deepest level of learning comes in *experience*. Knowledge, even spiritual revelation, becomes dead theology without the journey to conform to His image.

(70)

No one stands alone. Those whom you admire... know that they have a vast support team.

"A person standing alone can be attacked and defeated,
but two can stand back-to-back and conquer.
Three are even better, for a triple-braided cord
is not easily broken."
Ecclesiastes 4:12, NLT

(71)
It's good to stand out. You carry the Hope someone is searching the horizon for.

(72)

Obedience is always for a purpose, even if it makes absolutely no sense right now. Trust. Obey. Believe.

"Then you will experience God's peace,
which exceeds anything we can understand.
His peace will guard your hearts and minds
as you live in Christ Jesus."
Philippians 4:7, NLT

(73)
Contemplate love that looks beyond pain to victory...

"Let us hold tightly without wavering to the hope we affirm, for God can be trusted to keep his promise."
Hebrews 10:23, NLT

(74)
"You turn dark shadows
Into canopies of hope
And dry grass into gold.

My heart is spoiled and my breath consumed
When the beauty of earth gives a glimmer
Of understanding to the beauty of You."[5]

Sketch what this looks like to you.

(75)
So thankful for a God who likes one-on-one time.

(76)
You'll never find tomorrow in yesterday.
Harvest seeds. Kill weeds. Press on.

"Oh, that we might know the Lord!
Let us press on to know him.
He will respond to us as surely as the arrival of dawn
or the coming of rains in early spring."
Hosea 6:3, NLT

(77)

You will never fulfill your destiny until you know how purposefully God delights in you. His love draws up out of every pit and into His fullness.

(78)   Not sure which way to go?
Be still. Listen.
The Holy Spirit will lead you.
He's already prepared the way.

(79)
Jesus, I lean into You. When Your life flows through me, I am a part of what my Father is doing today.

(80)
Whatever your circumstance – whether in need or in abundance – may your heart remain thankful in all things, but hopeful in just One.

> "Let all that I am wait quietly before God,
> for my hope is in him."
> Psalm 62:5, NLT

(81)
Remember: Your true identity is in Christ.
He says you're amazing.

(82)

Don't wish for what used to be. In the Kingdom of God, movement is always forward: faith to faith, glory to glory. As you focus on Jesus, He will reveal the next step of faith; the next unveiling of glory.

(83)
If you let Jesus love you the way He *really* wants to, it will overflow and affect every area of your life. Love begets love. Beauty begets beauty.

(84)
Don't be afraid of being set aside for a season.

Growth in
difficult
places
produces
uncommon
beauty.

(85)
Iron sharpens iron.
In humility, the blades become the sharpest.

"As a prisoner for the Lord, then,
I urge you to live a life worthy of the calling you have received.
Be completely humble and gentle; be patient,
bearing with one another in love.
Make every effort to keep the unity of the Spirit
through the bond of peace."
Ephesians 4:1-3, NIV

(86)

Your Father God knows perfectly what you need, right now, in your current circumstances. If you believe this, it will affect the way you pray.

(87)

As love has always been God's motive and relationship His intention, you can expect to experience something personal.

Child

Friend

Beloved

Bride

"Do not fear, for I have redeemed you;
I have called you by name; you are Mine!"
Isaiah 43:1b, NASB

(88)
Faith is having the courage to look at the facts and choosing to believe the Truth.

"It was for freedom that Christ set us free;
therefore keep standing firm and
do not be subject again to a yoke of slavery."
Galatians 5:1, NASB

Endnotes

1   Litzelman, Amy Layne. *Deep to Deep*.
2   Litzelman, Amy Layne. *Again*.
3   Litzelman, Amy Layne. *How Can I Deny*.
4   Habakkuk 2:20. The Holy Bible, New International Version, NIV. Biblica, Inc.
5   Litzelman, Amy Layne. *This Beloved Road: Into the Source*. Jackson, WY: Window of Worship. 31.

Other books by Amy Layne Litzelman

This Beloved Road – A Journey of Revelation and Worship

This Beloved Road Workbook

This Beloved Road Vol. II – Into the Source

Diving Boards & Trampolines Vol. I

A Worshiper's Manifesto

www.ingramcontent.com/pod-product-compliance
Lightning Source LLC
Chambersburg PA
CBHW071724040426
42446CB00011B/2212